ANNE
ANDERSON

DOLLS AND WHY WE LOVE THEM

Dolls

AND WHY WE LOVE THEM

WELERAN
POLTARNEES

LAUGHING ELEPHANT BOOKS

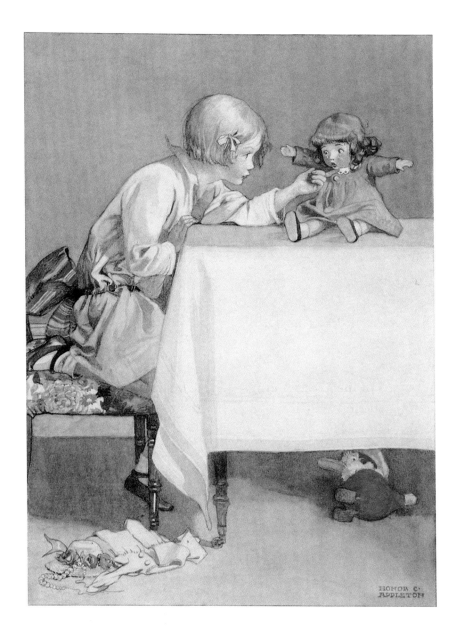

DARLING AND COMPANY   POST OFFICE BOX 4399   SEATTLE   WASHINGTON   98104

ISBN 1-883211-37-9

Early in childhood humans develop a fondness for small and helpless beings. It is instructive, and will develop into feelings that will make parenthood a joy as well as a responsibility. Young animals and babies inspire tenderness in most of us. We wish to touch and hold them, and we delight in their minature perfection. Even infants have this reaction, though it is less focused, being part of their delight in all life's manifestations.

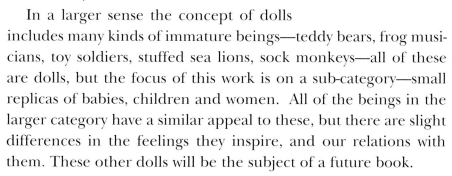

Dolls and toy animals draw upon this instinct. They appeal with their smallness and helplessness. They delight with their beauty.

In a larger sense the concept of dolls includes many kinds of immature beings—teddy bears, frog musicians, toy soldiers, stuffed sea lions, sock monkeys—all of these are dolls, but the focus of this work is on a sub-category—small replicas of babies, children and women. All of the beings in the larger category have a similar appeal to these, but there are slight differences in the feelings they inspire, and our relations with them. These other dolls will be the subject of a future book.

The innocence of dolls is invincible. Even when they encounter evil they fail to learn it. They have little or no knowledge of the larger world. They do not know that cats scratch, that fire burns, that busy streets are dangerous for small beings, or that rain will soak, and perhaps, destroy them. Without us they are lost. They are weak in abstract understanding—even of useful things like basic geography and simple mathematics—but they enjoy being instructed and informed; they slowly build a picture of their world, and are always grateful to those who teach them.

Most humans never find teaching as rewarding as the lessons with dolls, for even children can resist our enthusiasm, and disagree with our conclusions.

The beauty of dolls is of a very different kind than that of the humans they resemble. It is a simpler beauty. Mortal beings are infinitely complex in their physical selves. Their skin changes day to day. Their eyes water. Their mouths are constantly moving. Their moods are reflected in their faces, and someone who may be beautiful when in a good mood may be very ugly in a bad mood. If we like a doll's appearance we will probably always like it, for she has a fixed beauty which only very gradually decays with time, while we may change with the moment.

There is no disguising the fact that our need for power is one of the reasons we love dolls. We are their absolute monarchs, and they our totally obedient subjects. They go where we wish them to. They play as we wish to play. They dress in whatever fashion we elect. Even pets are not so docile. Where else in life can we be so central, so omnipotent?

Another, and pleasanter, way to look at our relation to dolls is to realize what opportunities for creativity they afford. Children, in particular, need opportunities to create in order to practice the arts of existence; all of us find creativity stimulating, but need opportunities. At every stage dolls invite us to create. They need names. They need to be clothed, and we probably have to design and make what they will wear. They need places to live. They will be satisfied with just a corner to sit in, but if we wish they will dwell in houses made with our hands and furnished through our ingenuity. They have no daily agenda, we must create it. They have no friends unless we introduce them. They know no games, but will gladly play those we invent. They cannot sing, or tell stories, but will listen patiently to anything we wish to sing or tell. They have, in and of themselves, rudimentary personalities, but it is up to humans to develop them in one direction or another. A lovely porcelain lady doll can be encouraged, for example, toward aloof vanity or warm graciousness. A rag doll can be foolish or wisely down to earth as we wish. Moreover, they can change in a moment, unlike us, and show a different face as our mood directs.

We love dolls for many reasons, but most centrally we love them because they need us so much, because they need us to fully live, and, if we love them as they deserve, they will give back to us a deepened capacity for love.

—*Welleran Poltarnees, Blue Lantern Studio*

When it comes to human babies we have no choices, but instead must accept what we are given. Dolls we can shop for, but this is a dangerous path for how can we leave behind a doll who cries out to us, how can we sort mercilessly through dolls who all need parents? It is much like buying a dog or a cat—we probably will wind up with the one who seems most to need us.

They're all of them so lovely
    It's very hard to choose.
I like that dark-haired beauty,
    With scarlet coat and shoes.

The golden-haired is sweeter,
    Her eyes are just sky-blue.
That sailor boy is cunning;
    The Highland laddie, too.

'Twould really be most puzzling
    To pick out only one.
(you see I can't have any,
    But choosing is such fun!)

—REBECCA DEMING MOORE

*I*t is best to be given a doll, for as elucidated on page four, choosing is morally perilous. We learn, if we are fortunate, that beautiful companions do not necessarily make the truest friends. When we receive a doll as a gift we are in the same position as the parents of human children who must accept the surprises of fate, and love whomever they receive.

receiving one's doll as a gift

"And what would you like as a present from me?"

"A doll."

"But I gave you a doll last Christmas and one for your birthday!"

"Yes."

"So you want to have many dolls?"

"Yes."

"Now tell me, what sort of dolls do you like best? Small ones or big ones? Baby dolls or dolls dressed as grown-ups? Soft dolls, wooden dolls, or . . ."

"Dolls please, just dolls to love!"

— BETTINA

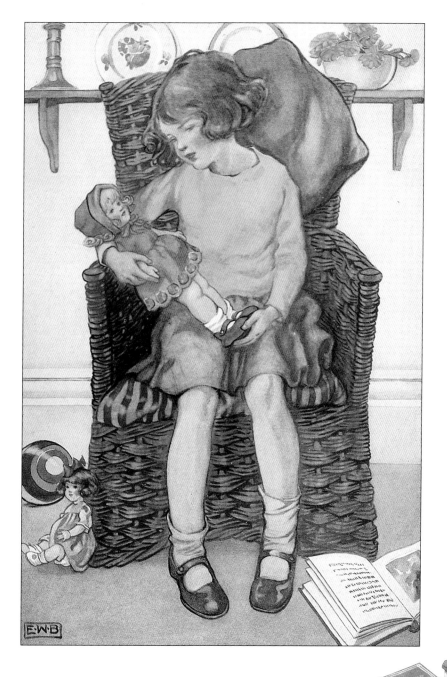

"She couldn't sleep. Which box held the doll? There were two boxes beneath the tree. Either could be the doll. One was flat on the starched white linen sheet in front of the tree; the other (you could barely see it) stood just behind the tree."

—SEON MANLEY

"What do you want for Christmas?" asked Kate's mother.

"I want a red ball," said Kate, "and a new dress and a book and a doll. I want a doll with golden curls who walks and talks and turns somersaults."

"Well," said Kate's mother, "we shall see what surprises Christmas brings."

—LIESEL MOAK SKORPEN

Melinda Jane, and Kate, and Nell
It's time you learned to read and spell.
Come, now, and say your A, B, C.
Hold up your heads, and look at me,
For, if you never learn to read,
What stupid dolls you'll be indeed!

—ANONYMOUS

GRAEFF.

*I*t is human to want to share our knowledge and enthusiasms with others. Dolls are the best of all audiences, for they know little of the world. They listen attentively to all that we have to say, and they want to please us by sharing our enthusiasms. Most dolls are like blank paper waiting to be drawn on, or mirrors waiting to be filled by a lively image.

teacher and pupil

When with my doll I play or walk
I'm very careful in my talk.
To keep one thing from her I strive,—
She shall not know she's not alive!

With grown-up people all about,
I'm so afraid the truth will out:
They might say things to let her see
She's not a real child like me.

And if she thought she could not think,
Or feel, or sleep, or eat, or drink,
Why, then, she would lie down and die,
Or else she'd cry, and cry, and cry.

—MRS. PERCY DEARMER

The central relationship we have with our dolls is friendship. Childhood is usually a time of spiritual isolation, for parents are too big and different, siblings are too competitive, and friendship with other children is usually more a matter of shared play than shared thoughts. We can tell our dolls everything, secure in their confidentiality and their unwavering affection for us.

*A*s with any beloved friend, we would like our dolls to be always with us. Only fear of the world's laughter teaches us to leave them at home, and makes them the secret companions of our most private hours.

the doll as constant companion

"The doll ate, and her eyes grew bright as stars. 'Have no fear,' said she. While I am with you nothing can do you harm. But remember—no one else must know of our secret. Now let us start."

—RUSSIAN FOLK TALE

"For the doll and child relationship is not as simple and crude as the non-doll-liker desires to think. Make no mistake—unless this happens to be the play of the moment . . . the child is not the parent of the doll, nor the doll the child of the child. For the very young the dolls can be the first really private and personal friend and ally."

—NAOMI LEWIS

$\mathcal{A}$ doll's passivity and size make it ideal for bathing. It is challenging to bathe a dog, and the bigger the dog the more difficult the challenge. Children are frequently reluctant bathers, and yet they enjoy bathing their dolls thoroughly, even mercilessly.

bathing one's doll

'Tis time Doll Rosy had a bath,
    And she'll be good, I hope;
She likes the water well enough,
    But doesn't like the soap.

Now soft I'll rub her with a sponge,
    Her eyes and nose and ears,
And splash her fingers in the bowl
    And never mind the tears.

There now—oh, my! what have I done?
    I've washed the skin off—see!
Her pretty pink and white are gone
    Entirely! Oh, dear me!

—ANONYMOUS

My dolly is a dreadful care,—

Her name is Miss Amandy;

I dress her up and curl her hair,

And feed her taffy candy.

—EUGENE FIELD

Creativity is a powerful impulse in humankind, and seems at its strangest in childhood when the act of making is a part of almost every life and every day.

Making doll clothes is a deeply satisfying activity, for the product is really useful. It is, of course, an exacting task, and if it is to be finely accomplished it almost always requires adult assistance.

"Long ago when the Doll Lady was a child, her only companions had been her dolls and one of those rare mothers to whom dolls are people. Every Christmas Mother dressed Lucile's family with infinite care:— 'Loved babies have hand-made clothes,' she would say, 'and so do loved dolls. You can always tell.' "

—LUCILE PHILLIPS MORRISON

COURT DRESSMAKER
DRESSES
COATS
BLOUSES

E.H.STEWART

A house is every doll's dream, though most girls do not even aspire to one, or even need one; for isn't the big house sufficient dwelling for the two of them. A doll's house does offer endless opportunities for play and pretending, even if it is only fashioned from a cardboard box. Here the doll is in charge. Here she can be the head of a family, rather than a very minor player. The child, who secretly rules it all from outside, tastes the glory and the responsibility of godhood.

a house for dolls

"Up in the nursery our largest plaything was the dolls' house. I cannot rid myself of the notion that it was built on a grander scale than any such house that I meet with nowadays – because I always have to stoop to look into their rooms, whereas the top floor of our house was just nicely on the level of our eyes. It had eight rooms on three stories: downstairs, on the left, was the kitchen, on the right the dining-room, with the staircase hall in between; upstairs, two bedrooms and a room which we sometimes used as the nursery, sometimes as the drawingroom, and, above these again, two attics. This mansion always seemed to promise a good spell of play. One of us would say: 'Hurrah, it's a real wet day. Let's play the whole morning with the doll's house.'"

—ELEANOR ACLAND

$\mathcal{H}$ealth and safety is one of the supreme concerns for mothers and fathers, and accounts for much of what children hear. "Are you sure you don't need a sweater?" "That's a very busy street. Look both ways." "You feel hot to me. I think you're running a fever." "You eat like a bird. I don't know how you survive." Children have neither the knowledge nor permission to turn the tables on their parents, but they do turn on their dolls the same scrutiny and are concerned in every aspect of their dolls' welfare and health.

dolls in poor health

"Mr. Puckler laid Nina on the table and looked at her a long time, till the tears began to fill his eyes behind the horn-rimmed spectacles. He was a very susceptible man, and he often fell in love with the dolls he mended, and found it hard to part with them when they had smiled at him for a few days. They were real little people to him, with characters and thoughts and feelings of their own, and he was very tender with them all. But some attracted him especially from the first, and when they were brought to him maimed and injured, their state seemed so pitiful to him that the tears came easily. You must remember that he had lived among dolls during a great part of his life, and understood them."

—F. MARION CRAWFORD

When we have tea I like to sit
And hold the pot and pour;
There isn't any tea in it—
But still there's always more.

And when I say, "You'll have some cream?"
Or "Are four lumps too many?"
They're so polite—they never seem
To know there isn't any.

An when an empty plate is passed
They gobble up the cookies fast.

—DOROTHY ALDIS

In the pleasant green garden
We sat down to tea;
"Do you take sugar?" and
"Do you take milk?"
She'd got a new gown on—
A smart one of silk.

We all were so happy
As happy could be,
On that bright summer's day
When she asked us to tea.

—KATE GREENAWAY

*T*eatime is an opportunity for a child to create order, to enforce rules, to dispense largesse. Some teas feature imaginary foods, some facsimiles of food made of clay, or paper, or whatever comes to hand, and some real food which all the humans share. An anonymous poet confesses "and when the dolls and I have a fine pretending tea / I put them all to bed, and then my tart is left for me."

Teatime is so traditional and resonant to the English mind that outsiders cannot understand its power in either a human or doll context.

ELSIE ANNA WOOD

$\mathcal{P}$lay is, with imitation, the foundation for a child's mental growth. It draws from the child both imagination and organization. It induces joy, contentment and confidence.

Play with other children is indispensable, but it dilutes each individual's contribution. Doll play is an opportunity for unhampered creativity.

dolls as playmates

"The imaginative child endues her doll with life, with reason, strangest of all, with temperament; in the subtle simplicity of a child's mind it is her child, with like reasoning powers and imagination. Who has not heard a child talking to her doll, living through the imaginary life of the puppet: the successes, the amusements, the sadness, the sickness, too, and the laughter, to say nothing of the naughtiness and the scrapes which have come within the experience of the child?

"Let a mother watch the pretended joys and sorrows which are the foundations of the games with the doll, and she will see the development of her little girl's mind more clearly than by much questioning, however confidential the relationship may be between herself and her little one. The child lends the doll her soul, the mind that is being born will be reflected accurately in the dollie's games."

—MRS. F. NEVILL JACKSON

"Of all such delights, the beauty of old dolls is the quintessential one. It has distracted me for years, leading me down remote and dreamlike paths to the disparate places where old dolls are to be found, introducing me to rare, magic people. Of my diffuse interests among the minor arts, none has been so rewarding as this obsession with the beauty of dolls."

—John Noble

*M*en and boys certainly do love dolls, though those that do are usually ashamed to make it public. The impulse for the miniature exits equally in both sexes. The imagination needs focus whether you are a boy or girl. Boys usually gravitate to toy soldiers, which are dolls of a certain kind.

The male sex's attraction to dolls can be surmised from the number of fine doll stories written by men, which include: *The Raggedy Ann and Andy Stories* by Johnny Gruelle, Richard Horne's *Memoirs of a London Doll* (1846), William Nicholson's *Clever Bill* (1926), Russell Hoban's *The Little Brute Family* (1966), Harold Jones' *There and Back Again* (1978), and Richard Kennedy's *Amy's Eyes* (1985).

The Encyclopedia Britannica points out that Mahomet played at dolls with his daughter, and that Cortez found Montezuma and his court playing with elaborate dolls.

$\mathcal{D}$olls play many roles in the emotional and developmental growth of humans, but the one they perform most frequently is just being there to be loved. Friends are mercurial, parents too frequently censorious, sisters and brothers preoccupied with their own place in the family, even pets have errands to run and wills of their own. Only dolls are always there, and always grateful for our love.

"For dolls are made for children, and deep in every doll there is a longing to be loved by a child."

—PAMELA BIANCO

JESSIE WILLCOX SMITH

loving one's doll

"We must specialize in describing this doll-love, for there are many varieties; the child who delights to fondle and mother her doll will have little love for the grand ladies, the courtiers, or freaks which inhabit the doll-world as well as the babies and little girls; probably the love of gay colors and dress, inherent in most children, has much to do with the pleasure taken in 'grand' dolls, while the pure doll-love which prompts another child to cherish her rough-hewn, shapeless 'baby,' and neglect the finely dressed lady doll is a separate and distinct variety of dollatry."

—MRS. F. NEVILL JACKSON

Your doll's cap has a frill of lace,
And her dress is flowered and fine.
Her hair isn't real, and her eyes won't shut;
But I love her 'cause she's mine.

— JANET DEXTER

*B*ed time can be frightening for people of any age, for there by our-
selves, in the darkness, all the fears we have hidden, all the doubts and
injuries we have concealed, are liable to leap forth and confront our
weakened selves. Adults can escape by turning on the light and read-
ing, or by waking a companion to converse, or by simply getting up and
driving away the fears and worries with action. Children are in a worse
state, for frequently they are forbidden to turn on the light, or resume
daytime activities. They must stay in the darkness and confront whatever demands may arise. In times like this, the best solution is a doll
to hold tight.

" 'Merry Christmas, Elizabeth,' said Kate as she tucked her into bed, 'and Happy
Birthday too! You are the best and most beautiful doll in the world, and I would-
n't swap you for anyone else.' "

— LIESEL MOAK SKORPEN

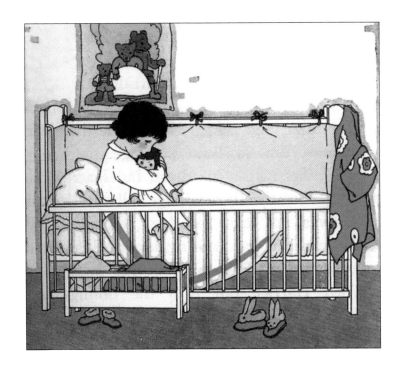

a child reading to an adult

I wash her hands
Till they are white,
And shine her cheeks
Till they are bright.
I tuck her in
So warm and tight,

Put up the screen
And fix the light
(She likes things done
EXACTLY right),
And kiss her nose
And say good night.

—DOROTHY ALDIS

PICTURE CREDITS

20	Harriet M. Bennett. from *Queen of the Meadow*, c. 1905.
21	E.H. Stewart. from *The Play Box*, c. 1911.
22	Frances Brundage. from *Little Darlings' Birthday Book*, c. 1910.
23	Unknown. from *Newlon-Hanna Speller*, 1933.
24	Unknown. from *The Prize for Girls and Boys*, 1910.
25	Anne Anderson. from *The Betty Book*, c. 1920.
26	Cecily Mary Barker. from *My Lovely Big Book*, c. 1936.
27	Elsie Anna Wood. from *Our New Story Book*, c. 1905.
28	Lucie Mack. from *Old Father Santa Claus*, c.1889.
29	E. Paterson. from *Dolly's Doings*, c. 1890.
30	E. Percy Moran. from *Rhymes and Stories of Olden Times*, 1894.
31	Lucie Mack. from *Old Father Santa Claus*, c.1889.
32	Sue Runyon and Ruth Bennett. from *Boys and Girls at School*, 1930.
33	Carl Larsson. "Självrannsakan," 1906.
34	Vera Stone Norman. from *The Lincoln Readers Primer*, 1926.
35	Jessie Willcox Smith. from *The Book of the Child*, 1903.
36	Marguerite Davis. from *Friends: A Primer*, 1929.
37	Torre Bevans. Magazine Cover, 1920.
38	John Rae. from *Lucy Locket: The Doll With a Pocket*, 1928.
39	Sarah S. Stilwell Weber. Magazine Cover, 1915.
40	Florence J. and Margaret C. Hoopes. from *The New Day in and Day Out*, 1948.
41	Hilda Cowham. from *Playbox Annual*, 1913.
42	Maud and Miska Petersham. from *Pleasant Pathways*, 1928.
43	Helen Jackson. from *Bonnie Bairns*, c. 1896.
Back Cover	Kate Greenaway. from *Little Patience Picture Book*, c. 1887.
Decorative Devices	Emanuel Hercík. from *Folk-Toys*, 1949.